Goodbye Love

The writings of a young man who knew what should befall him

David Chapple

Published 2010 by arima publishing
www.arimapublishing.com

ISBN 978 1 84549 445 2
© David Chapple 2010

All rights reserved

This book is copyright. Subject to statutory exception and to provisions of relevant collective licensing agreements, no part of this publication may be reproduced, stored in a retrieval system, or transmitted in any form or by any means, without the prior written permission of the author.

Printed and bound in the United Kingdom

Typeset in Garamond

This book is sold subject to the conditions that it shall not, by way of trade or otherwise, be lent, re-sold, hired out, or otherwise circulated without the publisher's prior consent in any form of binding or cover other than that which it is published and without a similar condition including this condition being imposed on the subsequent purchaser.

In this work of fiction, the characters, places and events are either the product of the author's imagination or they are used entirely fictitiously. The moral rights of the author have been asserted. Any resemblance to actual persons, living or dead, is purely coincidental.

Swirl is an imprint of arima publishing.

arima publishing
ASK House, Northgate Avenue
Bury St Edmunds, Suffolk IP32 6BB
t: (+44) 01284 700321
www.arimapublishing.com

Foreword

The author is a physicist who lectures in the OUDCE department of the University of Oxford.

But what is in this book is nothing to do with physics.

All the twenty four open verse writings in this book were written when he was a young man.

The writings express something totally different – something so sad and yet so beautiful.

Dare you read them?

Will you understand them?

The challenge is open to you …..

1. FOR ALWAYS

The leaves lie in their time, brown, brittle, deformed

A withered memory

The wind moves them always, giving them no peace in their death

They fall away into dust as she kisses them goodbye

These leaves are brown too

But these leaves are not withered and dried and cracked

They lie in their gentle suppleness because it has always been that way

And it is always their time

And the wind kisses them too

And I try to remember

And I try to remember and call back through the times and scan forward through the times, but the wind blows the mists of the times always

But I try to remember what I have to say and what I have to cry

And memories fade, and memories live, and I know them all so well

I guard them in the strong tower

Safe from the fierceness of the days and the nights, and kept from the kiss of the wind

So that she cannot say goodbye for always

But never kept safe from the times

And I try to remember about the embers as they glow

And I remember how the rain in her sweetness has cooled and will cool the hotness of their brow

And the wind will bear the ashes on her wings

But I forget as I try to remember because I am so old, and so young

One day in the warmth of the sun's love, when there were no shadows, and hearts were young

And her glistening reflections bounced off the bent corn in the gentle breeze, and the sweet sound of it rang and still echoes for always

I was there because I had to be

And as I remember the treasures, the treasures so priceless that only eternity can tell their story

I will remember for ever when the leaves were green

And I walked with them just yesterday

Again, along the lanes and streets of her fragrant times

And in the grove of dying trees, so long forgotten, the grey barks bow in their silence, and the little blackbird, still there after all these years, sings no more
And as the silence is torn by the cry of the everlasting wind
The brown leaves bear their own special fragrance of what they remember on her grey wings
And I will remember for always

2. YOU NEVER SAW

The yellow speckles of the sun's last lingering rays of the day scatter in the mist

And that which is lost is lost for ever

But the sounds begin to blend into that beautiful symphony as I close my eyes

The music is so faint, yet in its splendour gets slowly stronger as I listen, for these stolen moments

And their chords lift me away and carry me, as always, to the times of light

When two hearts touched and warm hands held, and love was alive in its wonder and warmth

But only I knew then, and only I saw the coldness ahead

And the times of darkness just beyond the dream

And for that moment in our time, borrowed just for then

You never knew what I know

And I wouldn't let you care about the pain I bore, because I never told you

But I said goodbye to you, every day as we flew together in the balm of the warm spring, over the meadows, smelling their fragrance

But only I treasured

Because only I knew that the winter was beyond

And I tried to tell you, to help you understand

But I knew you wouldn't treasure, and I knew you couldn't keep safe, that which was real for always

And so I said goodbye so many times

But you couldn't understand that some things are real for always

To be locked up in the strong tower

And that is why I could not give you the key

And those days were not real, just a medium

Given to me as I tried to cry to you

And tell you the story of that which had to be learned

And because you couldn't understand, is the reason why I was with you

But you were never with me, because you couldn't touch my heart

Because you didn't look for it with your life

But I saw your heart, in its purity, in its need, and its desperation

In its loneliness, and in its faithlessness and deceit

And I loved you because I had to

And as the sun kissed our skin, you were warm

But my heart felt the cold of the winter beyond our spring

That which is real must be laid hold of

And that which is true must be loved

And that which is for always must be treasured beyond the end

And the glistening yellow speckles in the cold mist turn darker as the sun falls away

And the howling of the winter's night wind whips and numbs

As I lie down and become still

The wings of the wind will carry the story of what was real for ever

And her howling cry will preserve its memory

Until the flowers blossom again

In the world of dreams

3. *LOCKED AWAY*

From my prison cell I drift away to my dreams to a land far away and another time

As the darkness rolls nearer, it doesn't matter

Because I fly away from it to the times where the sun paints the skies and her hair and her beauty

And my friend and lover the wind caresses my hair, and the balm of life in its sweetness I drink

And as I dance and as I fly across the fresh fields, we soar and rise, you and I, and fall nearer

And those sounds, my friends from those times, sing and chant to me and give me illusions of joy as I listen

And those sights and the sad smiles give me illusions of peace within, in my dreams

And as we walk the streets together, and as we play in the gardens together

We remember the warmth of that which we call love

And as we lie on the white sands as the sun says goodbye

The sea in its murmuring kisses our bodies and the moonlight bathes us in its balm

And our only pang is the end of the times, but not now

As long as there is life in that which is dying, the dreams will live again

And turn into reality for always and never fade away

For my dreams are our dreams and we will live them for always in our way

And as the snow blows in its purity we walk in it together

And you must cling to me, lest we be separated and slip away

And I lie in my stillness now in the white snow

And when a moment of our time has passed and the warm winds blow again

The brown leaves, dead from the trees, fall on me and cover me to help me say goodbye

Remember the colours and what they mean

And what they say

And as the blackness rolls nearer, I gaze out of my prison cell over the hills in the distance

The secrets are mine, and they are locked up with me in my isolation

Safe for all of the time

And who is the keeper of the golden key?

4. THAT DAY

My world is the world of the wild wind and the waters flow there too

No one knows what the wind or the waters speak of except me

The wind is sometimes silent, but she is there in the distance

When she sings to me, her song is a song of sadness

She moans gently and cries of her devastation

But sometimes I fly on the wings of the wind, with her, being caressed by her fragrance, her coldness, her loneliness

I am her servant when I choose to be but she always wins at the end of times

Because she speaks of death, the death of light, happiness and life

And she speaks of times

Her story remains untold, except to me, because I understand her

What she means, and why she cries

One day when the waters roll in their coldness I will remember it all

The bright lights and the sounds of wonder

The wind doesn't know that I have won

Because these lights cannot fade away now

Nor the sounds grow quiet

I have no choice and so it will be, in my heart, in the majesty of eternity

Until the leaves of time fade away

The waters reach and destroy, so slowly, but I stand, silhouetted against that mixture of darkness and light with all its changing dimensions

Until the birds sing no more and the gentle breeze whispers no more for always

And I stand alone because I stand untouchable

Out of reach of the world with its deceit and glitter, emptiness and echoing hollowness

Only the wind knows me, and the waters are my gentle friend and distant enemy

But as they rock me I sway them in all their knowledge of the past

Because I know it too

And as the world rolls along and screams its mad, sad song

I stand above it all, and I stand alone

And the world rolls away and recedes into the distance far, far removed
And yet it is ever near, to be toyed with in some wasted moment or other
The waters are ever deeper and grow darker with their depth
And an unknown world lies there, to take or to leave
And yet I stand, with the vista of timelessness and all it has meant, locked away,
Protected to perfection, alone with me
Until that day

5. *SHADES OF DARKNESS*

And when the night comes, my friend, I close my eyes with such gladness and such sorrow, and I drift away

To escape from the hauntings of this day and its circles of hollowness, I drift away

And in that other place, which I share with no person

The wind kisses your hair and your cheeks

And it cuts and hurts you with its howlings

No person, except me, because I am there, and I see you and I listen to the wind

My old friend, from the times

And we both feel the rain as it falls so gently in that place

I am there, but you can't see me, because I am in the hidden places

And my story remains untold

In this place you forget the howlings and the screamings of the nightmares from within

And the unbearable pain

And the hurt which torments me, I try to run away from

In this world of dreams, where the corn bends softly in the wind

And the blackbird, in the decaying branches of the dying trees, sings a new song to you
This is the song of life for you
Listen to its sounds and its echoes from over the oceans of time
Because it speaks of the hidden times that I know so well
And as the closeness of the dream begins to fade and its beauty dies you must awake again to face that which you do not know
But that which haunts you, you know so well in your heart
And as the relentless and merciless noises of the world devastate your mind and heart again
You will remember me, because I have spoken to you and I am there
Treasure the wind, and bind its secrets to your heart, for always

6. SO SORRY

I just wanted to tell you, that's all

About flying away borne on the wings of that love that the wind speaks of

When she blows, caresses, moans, lifts, carries away

She cools down the hot anguish and the twisting turmoil that never ceases, as she kisses our brows

She will never forget, because my story has been taken by her and treasured for all time now

And she sings it sweetly and sadly in the skies

With no one to listen any more

She will treasure the moments and the years

And I go to her and fly in her arms, just to be near her

Because she has listened and understood and treasured

And every time I climb in her lofty towers, I am alone with her and the memories.

I just wanted to tell you, that's all

About the cost of life, and of giving and of loving with that deepest love

So deep that it cannot die

I just wanted to tell you about the burdens and the darkness, and the end
And what happens to that love then
But I've told you, and somewhere in some far reaches of some kingdom's skies
If you fly on her wings, and listen carefully
You may hear the story again, and its wonders, and its tears, and its pity, and its strength, and its death, and its life
Go there one day, search the skies, because I will be searching them too
And don't give up, never in all your days
Until you find the treasures from another time
The wind is pure, and she doesn't say goodbye
And she will never leave
And soon she will comfort the hotness of my sorrow
As I turn to rest in her sweetness, and her coldness
And I give the treasures and the memories to her to cry upon
So that she can wail their sad song, until you hear it again one day, clearly, for always
I just wanted to tell you, that's all

7. AGAIN

The grey gathers in the sky and hangs in its motionless sleep

And yet the north wind blows today in all its chill

And as it blows cold I look through it as it cuts my eyes, and makes the tears run along my head

But I don't need those eyes to look through the grey

And as I stand there alone, as always

I hear the continuous sounds of life in our little world that surrounds us

I see the glittering sights of its transience and smell its familiar messages

As I tilt back my head

But the sounds are echoes, and the sights are images of that which leads to nowhere

And yet, you must tread that path this day

And as I cut through the grey, I drift away

And I fly to another time and another place

And we were there together once, and we will be there one day again in dreams

And we must try to be together then

And we slip along the streets together

And the west wind blows its fragrant balm across our heads

And the sun kisses our joy and our peace with its warmth

And I look upon us both and I live again the fragrance of our great and beautiful love

And I lie down in the soft fields as I watch you there

And those who must watch over us with their love and their care are there

And we hear the sounds of real life

And we see the sights of wonder, and we smell the balm of truth in our time

But above us the blackbird sings its song of sadness even then

And the sun turns red as it begins to set, so far away

And as I reach and touch the tenderness of its memory

The north wind cuts me deeper as I fall on the cold ground in the other time

And as I lie down alone, as always, I say goodbye again to that which is life

And that which is love

And that which is pure, and I slip away into the other times

And the grey caresses my head and body with its coldness now
And light turns into darkness
North wind, my old friend and enemy, blow upon me
And darkness, beset me about
Phantoms of the blackness, hunt and destroy me
In the strong tower, that which is precious is locked away for all time
And that which is real is there
And I will remember again

8. FEARS I DARE NOT FACE

The coldness and the bleakness of the winter cuts, hurts, shrills and drills deep

But it can't hurt me

It cannot penetrate the barrier and the shell of my eternal prison

My prison is my strong fortress to protect me

It insulates me from my deepest, darkest fears

Nobody sees through my shell, and I am safely locked away inside

How long will it be before my strength fails?

Cracks appear in my strong tower

Oh cold winter which spells out death in the last analysis, will you penetrate?

Will you pull me down in my loneliness?

No one sees my loneliness –

But the spring – the eternal spring, must blossom in my heart

When you blossom oh sun of solutions

I will not need my ivory tower anymore, for then I will be fulfilled

But spring, when her time is done, fades away

Her flowers die, her leaves decay, fall, are swallowed up in emptiness

If you dawn upon me, sun of fulfilment, will you leave me again?

When spring turns to autumn, what sad beauty is the beauty of decay

The hue of colours and the carpets of green, blue and red, give way to the icy winds of eternal loneliness

Will you chill me oh winds?

Will you be my constant companion?

Because you start to chill me even now

Oh answer to my deepest dreams, will you elude me?

I fear you will

Because my dreams are no ordinary dreams

And they are special, treasures of priceless worth

What sun can fulfil them?

If I am fulfilled, then darkness will appear on the horizon

All the rainbows will fade away

All the sunsets will be lonely

For you will never, never return my love

In all eternity

9. THE LONGEST JOURNEY

The bareness of the land is so wide

No flicker of a soft wind blows to caress the sadness of the heat

The journey home is long and weary in the darkness

And the lights are dim in the distance

But they draw nearer

Chill winds blow now and cut me to the core, but still I walk onwards, sometimes stumbling

But always climbing up again

Until the time comes to give up

In the barren land, I pass through the valley of loneliness and emptiness

But still I see the faint lights of home

There is only one home for me, for always

I cannot rest or survive in any other place

But there are so many rivers to cross and mountains to climb on the way

But I have climbed all my mountains

And forded all my streams

And still the cold wind blows, and creatures of the loneliness howl to me of despair as I pass by

One more hill, one more stream, one more bend, and the lights of home are there

I smell the fragrance and hear the echoes that will be with me for eternity, and that is locked in my life for always now

The gates are firm and the doors of stout cedar are locked

The windows are barred and shuttered, but the devastating light still streams from the cracks

Will the doors remain shut to me for always

Or will the golden keys turn in the locks of hardened steel?

So that I may enter in at last, locking the doors behind me

Until even the leaves of time fall from her eternal tree?

10. WINTER

The trees begin to bend a little bit as the first colder winds begin their sad song

And the coldness comes today as that which is life begins to fade

But although it fades, a trace of its beautiful colours can still be seen, as the haunting hollowness of this winter gathers in

Those colours, once bright in their vibrancy, echo the memories of so many parts of the times

Our times

And the tender fragrance of their balm is still sweet in the evening as the birds become silent

For so long that bird has sung its song of love and hope and joy and sorrow, and it is still there

Though the time for the singing to end is near

And the cold winds sing their song of sadness, as they moan in the hills

And while the last remnant of the warmth of the times of life say goodbye

And there are no more leaves to fall in their death from the trees, now so old

And so barren in the wind

I fly away into that other land and that other time of dreams that have been, and I see you there

And we laughed and sung, and we ran

Panting by the silver spray of the sea

And we flew over the lands of yellow corn swaying in the gentle breeze

And I see you there in all your loveliness

And our ears heard the sounds of life

And our hearts beat so strongly because of that which had to be lived and loved

And the winds blow and cool my head as they call me back to this time when the last winter sets its seal on the land

And as the wind becomes harsher in its beating, and as the coldness tries to penetrate into the secret places

That heart gets fainter, but only because of the darkness that is coming

And the trees, bare black shadows stripped of life now, against the dark background, rock and bend as the wind screams its message

Blow oh wind, and destroy

Beat down oh rain in your newness of power, and drown that heart in its sorrow

But I drift back through the ages in my heart and I know the secrets

They are mine, and they will stay with me, locked up and treasured for always in the secret place

And as the cold earth becomes white with winter's snows

I will remember for always

11. I DIDN'T HAVE A CHANCE TO SAY GOODBYE

I knew, so long ago, before we ever met, that we would say goodbye one day

One day when the sun hid her face and the sky went black

I knew before you were born that the end would come in all its sorrow

And that is what the wind has said all through these years

In its sad moaning over the hills and as it cries its song of goodbye through the trees after the sun sets

And when the moon casts her ghostly shadows

Shadows of love and shadows of life

But now is death and goodbye

Goodbye my sweet dream and my precious love

Fly away on the wings of your wind

Your wings have healed now, after all these years

And you fly back to your forest

Back to your kind

And never let so much as a thought of those days cross your mind or touch your heart again

Those days when the sun shone in her warmth, and blessed our hands and our hearts

But we both knew about goodbyes, and you never gave me a chance to say my goodbye

And as you fly in God's heaven through the clouds and near to the wind, listen carefully

Because the wind will carry my story to you there, for that is where I will be

And she will say goodbye for me

But I will remember for always

12. IT TAKES SO LONG TO TELL YOU

Here I go, slipping away

Into eternity

There is nothing I can do about it now

All those I love with my life are there

And they drift away

They get smaller as we get further away

It is the time for saying goodbye for always now

Although that time has always been there for me and for

them with respect to me

I love them all with a love so profound

So devastating, so frightening, that it must carry through into

eternity

I can't die or wane in my heart, only grow

Stronger, deeper, the essence of life

But coldness now

Darkness is coming

And you are there

I know it because I can see you and feel you leaving me

Did I tell you?

Did I tell you what I have to say?

Did I tell you properly about the times and about love so strong?

The burden of my life and my heart

I had to tell you

I had to scream it from a mountain top

I had to let somebody know what happened, all that time ago, now and for always

But did I tell you?

Did you give me the chance?

It takes such a long time to tell it

It takes lives, lifetimes

It can't be told by words, only muttering mumblings – tools which fail me

My hope is, and my knowledge, that your mind would transcend my words and you would understand

You have to understand

You could have understood

But did I tell you?

Did you give me the chance?

The time?

There is nobody else in this world that can tell it – only me

I am the only one who knows because I lived through it

And I know you too

So well

The first day I ever saw you I knew everything about you, but you didn't.

I have to tell somebody

I have to tell you

If I die and don't tell it, it will die with me

Goodbye all of you

Goodbye you

I love you with everything for always

The coldness

The finality

The darkness

The last glimpse of the light as it recedes

The silence

The silence

The silence

The silence

There is no one to hear it, or understand it anymore

The precious treasures I had to give

The knowledge

The depth

The warnings

The answers

The horror and devastation of what had happened all that time ago, so long ago

And what will happen to you some time

There is no one to tell it anymore

Did you give me time to tell you?

Did I tell you?

13. THE LAST ILLUSION

Through the heat and the dryness, I stagger on

Towards the rocks, which have always hung on the horizon

They have never got larger, but have always stayed the same,

in the distance, so far away

The clock of time ticks, and the ticks echo silently, loudly

But the grey rocks have loomed larger for a while now, as my

approach draws nearer

That means that the journey is coming to its end

And I turn my head and try to look back

The vista behind me is misty

And the fogs of time and the times swirl and tell me that the

journey behind me is an illusion

And parts of it I can see

But the grey mists enter my mind

And make it so hard to remember and to think

There is no peace now and cannot be again

As I wrestle with the persistent ache of the fight

I give up now and quit

Ahead of me are the rocks

And I know that on the other side of them are my phantoms that wait for me
To haunt me for always
I have tried to shut them out and dismiss them, but they manage to break through in the darkness of the night when I am so alone
And they confront me
The cry that has sounded from the earliest of the times will die
Because it is dying
The tenderness and love that filled the void in the beauty of imagination is beginning to sleep, fitfully in its hardness
And the rocks in their austerity threaten the sun's light as they rise on the horizon
Let us switch out the light now
While there is still time
And let the fields be green again
Swaying in the balm of the sweet breeze
And let life be young again as the sun sparkles on the streams

Because here are the beauteous memories of the times of wonder

And the times of you, mystical creature

Wherein is love and wherein is life

But illusion recedes so quickly, and I can't switch out the light any more

The light which sears into the dark recesses revealing the stark nakedness and fullness of the reality and the truth

The times were never fulfilled, were they?

I will need you to help me through the darkness

Because I fear the phantoms, one day

One day be there without vanishing away

The last illusion of all

14. THE BEARER OF DREAMS

I see a new world today

Where the sun's soft warmth falls again after the coldness of the dark winter

And her rays of life burn away the signs of the winter's bleak death

Feelings return to that which had lost life

And the warm birth of a new chance lives once more

The fading colours fall away

And the empty hollowness of death echoes are swallowed up in the light

And will the long grass sway in the warm wind again today?

And will the fragrance of new times be borne on her wings again?

But as my eyes turn away from the vision, just a little bit, the new world fades away

And gives way to the other world which permeates the complement of it all

Other world creatures cry and move and lie in their stillness

And their hauntings echo across the black night

And pierce through the mists of delusion

Awakening those who would slumber and dream

But who is the bearer of dreams?

And who is the teller of the true story of life?

The bearer of dreams knows the truth

And the thunder of the future beckons from the end of times

So run, lest a chill wind cut your heart

And drive a way through the black shadows

Into the distant brightness, where dreams of your new world walk and talk

Listen to the laughter of the waves in the warm morning

And the songs of the young spirits

And lose yourself in their curious fantasy

Because the illusions of the other world you must escape, until the time

Until the time when you must try to remember

And if you remember, then you will remember the bearer of dreams, so long ago

When he came with the potion of truth in his cup

Find the cup, lying in its corruption and drink from it if you can

Because the cup is hard to find, and dreams will all fade away

And the young spirits will grow old

But you will remember me

15. DRIFT ON

Released again to wander through the oceans of time, I drift on

Sometimes passing by familiar places which I remember

Hidden and uncharted are the times, some of them tender

Some bitter

Some beautiful

Some treacherous

But all are precious because they are the times

And the wandering is precious too because you might listen

And you might hear what I have to say

My howling, and my cryings in the dark times and in the light

Never able to stop at land in these oceans

Except for a few moments on the shore

Until the winds caress my sails and move me away

And their sad moan says goodbye for me

And I say goodbye as well

I always say goodbye, but never to the wind

The storms appear on the horizon, so many times and they lash me

And their forces are always set against me, one after another, and together
The hard bullets of rain beat me and try to hurt me
But they pass on
And when I breathe in the clear fresh air, the gentle rain runs down me and tries to take away the pain
My sweet friend and comforter
You and the wind are my companions through all the times
And I remember you because I knew you so long ago, when you were just the same as you are now
So alone and so frightened of the world and what it might do to you
And yet, nostrils high, head flung back, facing it
And looking for that which you must have and cannot find
But you know you cannot find it in your heart, and you tell a lie to your heart
But your heart, beating so heavily and so fitfully knows the only truth
And I know the truth because I knew you so long ago
Before this part of our times began
As I drift further into the night, I remember you

And you will remember me for always

Because the wind you will hear will be my message to you

And the rain falling gently on your cheeks my touch

Which you have longed for, for so long

And as the ocean of time ticks on into eternity, cry for always

16. WHILE THERE IS STILL LIFE

The clouds drift by, getting darker

Always they get darker

Sometimes letting the silver light shine through in their breaks

Even the silver gets darker, as the day dies

It dies in its profound silence, yet its silence is only an echo of the noise of the times

Those sounds that have worn away and taunted and chanted and moaned and screamed

They all lay silent now

Not you though

Not you

I don't want those sounds to follow you and overtake you in your day

Because your day is your time, and mine has overlapped

Like the intersection of sets into yours

The intersection is shared by those lives

But the sounds are there too

The sounds will not die away until the time comes when they grow fainter

When they begin to die, life is dying and will not revive any more

The sounds are the sounds of life in its death throes

And the fading silver of the dying day says goodbye again as always

Reminding of the future when the darkness comes for always

The breeze blows gently too, sometimes chilling in its cool honesty

And sometimes caressing those days with its warmth

Try to remember

Try to remember

Try to remember the silver breaks in the fog of your mind

When the breeze cuts through

Cool and pure

And the vista of reality pours itself upon those days

Please never shut down the towering walls of a wonderful mind on those truths

Because those truths are life

And I feel the pain of your cries as I pant

Powerless and unable to clarify

Without strength to spread the salve

The balm of solution to the tragedy

And even though I am so tired now, because of the sounds

And because of the light

I cry in the deep places

Because I try to remember

And I try to remember, while there is still life

And while there is still silver

Help me to remember

17. THROUGH THE WINDOW

The long pains of many days linger in my bones and in my heart

The harshness of another winter is over now, but not for me

The birds in your spring time sing their first new song of life and warmth and love

But they are in your world, not mine

I look and listen for the last time as life ebbs

And death catches up with me

And I see your world and listen to its sweet sounds

And as our worlds separate after all our years and all our lives

The wind sings again to me

I fly on her wings now, but soon she will bear me on them and carry me to my world for always

And she sings a song to me

Her song cries as it moans in the tree tops

And only the wind and I know the story

She caresses me again with her coldness and numbs me gently

As gently as she can, into that long sleep where the pain will go away, but always linger

But all the time she will love me

And she will remember

And always she will bear me up in her anguish

And her frenzy and her storms and her rainbows

And as the mists around my mind and my eyes come closer

And as the pain burns deeper

I look again through the window which separates your world from mine

And I see you there in all your loveliness

Always alone, unable to touch me as I reach out to you

Because our window keeps us apart, as it has always done

And I love you as I have always done

But you don't see me, as you never have

Because you can't

And I remember us together in the fresh fields, in the sun and in the rain

In the heat and in the cold

Together but always separated

And I can still feel, even now at the end, the sun's warmth on our bodies

And on our hearts

And the winter's bitterness

And I held your hand in the winters, but you didn't know I was there really

Because you never could see me

And the balm of our summers still smells fresh in my nostrils

As the corn rocks in the breeze

And as the trees bent in the winters when the wind cried and screamed her warnings

She said goodbye for us

And now the dying fragrances of autumn linger as life decays in my world

And soon the window will be darkened and I won't see you any more

But you will be safe now in your world

And spring will begin again for you

And I press my lips to the window to try and kiss you and to touch you

To say goodbye again for the last time

And the pain burns in my bones and in my heart, as always

And the birds and the new flowers, and the new lives

And the new springs, and the new sun will soon forget me

And as I try to settle for and settle in the coldness and the darkness

And as our window fades away into eternity

I know that I will remember for always

18. NOBODY KNEW

As the night carries me away, alone

Into my secret places

I cry as the darkness deepens

Then I rest from the labour of living out the day and the night

And I look for peace from the ache of trying

But nobody knows

And I become myself then, in my isolation from the world

And I fly away on my dreams

To a distant place where I am alone

But the winds are warm and balmy

And the wind blowing there crackles the leaves with laughter as I stand there

Free from the shackles

But nobody knows

The southern zephyr caresses my head as the years go by

And I am frightened to think of life

And scared to dream of that which is real and that which is beautiful

Lest I cry and can never stop

But nobody knows

And as I walk through the shores

The warm water laps around my feet and comforts me

As its silver spray blows over me

And for once I am real and I live and I love

But the dawn is coming

And I flee to the darkness of the night where I live in my heart

But its silver rays overtake me

And as I rise to another day

I say goodbye to my tears of crystal and my golden dreams

And I put on my face and dress in my actor's clothes and face another day

With its nothingness

Because nobody knew

And nobody cared

Except you

19. *FIVE THINGS*

I turned my eyes away from the deepest darkness

Because I thought I sensed, saw, a faint light

But it was only a memory

Deceived by its form I gazed for a time

And I saw with hollow eyes, filled with sorrow

And in the memory I saw five things

The first was an image of beauty

Bathed in a wonderful light

Which danced around and off the colours of that which was once a dream but which had now gone away

The second was a glimpse of life, which had flickered for a while

And then died

The third was a picture of her

Bright and shining in the radiance of her beauty

She danced a sweet dance of youth, love, and gladness

Smiling and telling me even then that she remembered what would be

What would come to pass, and what we would go through

I danced with her smile, and moved closer

And mirrored it on my lips
Trying to let go and hoping to be lulled into another world
On the wings of a lullaby
We danced together then, for always it seemed
But I knew it was only for a moment, while my soul and my heart beat all that there was
And all that was left
Her silken dancing clothes of mist and fresh dew wrapped me in their gentle swirls and carried me away
And we saw what shouldn't be seen
And yet which should
And we played happily in the tender green fields of time
And on the shores of the sea of sorrow
But we didn't look at the sorrow then, just felt its pull
We flew away but never very far
Into the valleys where balmy fragrances of tenderness and sweetness were borne on the wind
Because the southern zephyr blew across the land
Healing in its path with the breath of comfort on its wings
I was there with you and we danced and danced until we came to the gardens of love

Where I laid down alone and cried alone for always

I wanted to stay in the gardens because I was looking for you again

But you had gone and I didn't know where

O birds of the air carry my message

Mountains beyond hear my cry and tell it on the wind

But I could still smell her fragrance

Touch her beauty and whisper her name

But I never saw her again

Sometimes I thought I heard her singing in the distance, but it was always the wind

Whistling softly in the high leaves

I was always deluded

And yet I never learned the truth in my soul

The fourth was a heart

A stout heart this one

Beating so strongly in one so poor

One so broken and one so young and yet so old

And I looked at the heart and saw strength and weakness

Pity and sorrow

It heaved with its torture of burdens and time

And as I looked it began to slow

To lose its pace, to die

The fifth was a tree, old, gaunt and withered

It looked ghostly as it stood alone against the background of the azure sky with its coldness

The tree held many secrets, of life and of death, because as seasons came and seasons went, it gave birth to new leaves and let them live again

It let them breath in the warmth of their short lived spring

And enjoy the heat of their summer

And it said goodbye to them all as the sun said goodbye

Each leaf waving goodbye to the tree as it left with a last kiss

When it was so cold in its withered brown shell

No resilience was there any more

Just the brittle dryness of the end

As it fell to its place on the ground

Soon it wouldn't even be a memory any more

And would never be seen again

But this tree could bear no leaves again

Because it had been stripped of its bark

And had died so long ago

And yet it stood, still tall, stretching upwards as if trying to touch the heavens
And as I drifted closer, drawn inevitably to the tree
I saw its body was hollow now
What are those sounds I hear, whistling through its dead branches?
They are the sounds of a memory of something so precious
Like a glistening tinkling
As clear waters scatter on their path through the mountains
That is the voice of a love, so deep, so immense, so wonderful, that it can't be contained
The silver river of that love, as it flows in its unstoppable majesty was the beat of that heart
And the life of those leaves
And what of the dream, what became of it?
It dreams on
Never doubt as it lifts in its loveliness
And I will return to remember, one day

20. *YOU WILL REMEMBER*

The sounds carry through the air

Just like they have done for a long time

Just for a moment

But tomorrow they won't be there

And in their times what have they seen?

They have seen the teacher of love's end

And the students learning how to say goodbye

Some couldn't learn, some didn't want to learn

But some learned well

All these things lie silent now

Because, as at the end of every holocaust and every phase

The winds and the sounds blow away the voices

And the faces, sometimes smiling, sometimes sad

And they try to blow away the memories

But the real memories remain there

The memories of what has been real and what has been true

They will never leave this place

Even when its dust sinks into the sodden earth

And I will visit this place again one day and one night

And so will you

And I will sing to you the song of mourning

And it will be sweet to your ears

And you will remember how we listened to the sounds

And breathed in the essence of that age, together

And none of us knew what was happening

Save that I gave you my arms beneath you

To try to hold you up

And the nights came, and the days, and the coldness, and the heat

And the total transience of that place

But you learned so much because I taught you so much

But you learned so little

And soon this sanctuary will end

Because I cannot live here any more

Because of you, then and now

And so it will cease to be

And who will know?

Will they feel the racing heart, who must come here tomorrow?

Will they know the story in a moment or two?

As I pack again my transient bag, and leave

I will carry for always the fragrance that was there, with you

But the fragrance that will remain will be the puzzle

And the mystery, and the haunting to those who come

But when we return we will be alone

And we will drink in the majesty of our times

And then we will fly away together, and we will hold each other's hand as we soar

And when we reach the far away place

In the end

Then you will remember how to say goodbye

21. SOMETHING BEAUTIFUL IN THE DARKNESS

Something beautiful in the darkness

I can see it and I can feel it

How tender and precious it is in my heart

It is locked away from the ravages of the world and the time

in my strong tower

And I will always remember it

And as the perpetual darkness pervades, as it always does

And as it always has for so long now

That precious thing of beauty is there

I am so glad and so sad that it is there

For how can a red rose live in the desert

When the dry winds come and blow across its tender petals

And how can it live when the sun in its harshness beats down

upon its tenderness

Wild beasts and predators will come and devour it

And trample it under foot

Its roots grow down, but it finds no drink

How can it live?

Something beautiful is fragrant in the darkness

I will give food and drink if I can to your red rose

I will try and preserve it from its predators

But I am so old now, and so choked with the darkness

How can I help it when there is no light and no clearness?

I will cherish it in my heart and lock it up for always

And I will remember it

And when the darkness deepens

And time slows down

And the weary noises of the world have gone away for always

I will remember, for always, how that something beautiful

struggled for its life in the midst of death

May it live and never die

Preserver of beauty

22. ONE DAY, FAR , FAR AWAY

The world is still beautiful, if you look carefully

At the right time in the right places

Although the light reflected off the fields and the sun

glistening off the sea seems a little dimmer

And the sounds of life a little quieter

It's so long now, almost as if I lived it before

Knowing how it would always be, the end always there

There only ever was a chance

Just the fleeting moments in which to tell of life and love

It's over again now, just as it was in the beginning

Just as I lived with since the beginning

And tried to tell it and sing it as sweetly as I could every day

And there were days when I couldn't sing my song

When I just had to pretend to believe it wasn't there

And I had to pretend to die

And so did you

But the sun is dimmer now

And its rays seem to be more golden

Instead of burning brightly as if they know they are saying

goodbye too

The wind was strong today as I walked in it, facing it

Cutting through it, as it tried to hold me back

But it was warm and comforting

Yet cold and harsh, as it helped me say goodbye

What happened to that which we called love?

To that fearful link and bond?

That frightening yearning and eternal blaze which held us so close and so tight?

As I say goodbye to you and to our love

I cherish every moment, every memory and every dream and beat of our hearts

And my heart will always beat with yours and will always be yours

And I know that when tomorrow comes

If it comes

You will be there, with me, through the days, in the rain

Through the storms, in the dark cold night as well

And when I stand alone

In some lonely place

Facing the wind and the rain, with darkness around me and in me

You will be there in my eyes, in my dreams, and in my heart

And I will remember that I loved you, and you loved me too

And we told each other secret things that would only be said and heard just once in all of time

And I will remember your smile, your smell, and just you

And the memories will hurt me and haunt me

And I will not let them go

Because they are ours for always

And nobody else can have them or share them

And as we say goodbye to our love

Please forgive me for the parts that hurt

And please treasure that which must never be lost

The world is still beautiful, but not for me today

And as I try to lay down now

And, broken, I stumble on to my knees, the wind forcing me down

I tremble with the cold, and whisper my prayer on the wind

That one day, in a time and a land far away

We will be together again for always

23. *THAT HEART*

The sun sets and sheds its fading glory for the last time

The sun says goodbye and its warmth kisses that hand for the last time as it slips away

The darkness that will be left is no stranger to that life

Because that life has lived with the death of life for always

And that mind slips away into the past now

For always it slips into the past until

And those eyes see again

They see the fresh smells and felt the new and tender fragrances that woke

And the delicate silken thread of love, the only love, shines in the sunlight

And the heavens smile down upon the newness of the wonder

And its age

And the intimate beauty, undiscovered, and yet such an old friend

Lingers for that moment, which is for always

It has to be for always

And those lips will cry out for ever

As long as they can tremble, the story, and the glory of those times
Those times that flashed across the vista of that life for a fleeting instant
And yet for always
And those feet walk with those feet
And they follow
And they follow
And they have always followed
And always led
And the calmness and safety of the promise
Those arms embrace for all the times
Goodbye now sun, and as those hands let go of the last warmth,
That frame stands alone again, as always
And wails for the other old friend, to caress and blow in its chillness against that head
And as the wind blowing in the deepening darkness howls and cries again,
And as eternity gathers together again,
The rain falls and soothes and moistens

Blow oh wind, and sting oh rain

Rise oh waters and overcome, and bear away the treasures if you will

The strong tower keeps her secret

And the hidden treasures remain through it all

And for always

In that heart

24. SHUT DOWN

And there as I turn the last bend

The dusk falls

And its shimmering starlets scatter the last light

The magic rainbow fades as it slips away over the edge into the emptiness

Taking the pot of gold, which I never saw

The elusive pot of gold, which was never worth the chasing

Is gone for always

And the damp mist smells sweet to my nostrils tonight, as I shut down

After the end of the long trip, switching off everything

Reluctantly in the half light

And considering that just a few moments ago, it seemed

I started out

Used a lot of fuel, came a lot of miles, wore a lot of track,

Did a lot of damage, told a lot of truth

Hid a lot of hurt,

Said goodbye always

In all those years

And with the engine resting, I lay back and remember the dust

And the storms that I passed through

And although I was never with you, you were with me

In that deepest way, in my heart

From the beginning

Before the times

And I knew you then, as I know you now

So frail, so sad, so poor, totally alone

But before you fade away, as I release my grip on the wheel

I try to look again at you

And I have to tell you of that which nobody knows

But which you have to know

Because it is the essence of your life and of your days

You shone in your sunshine

And your hair glistened, and your eyes sparkled

But nobody knew why

And those who saw it saw the wrong thing

And some thought you shone for them

But nobody understood your pain

As you tried to win

But you have to know that you didn't lose in the end

Because I saw

And before the times I knew, and I felt it all for you

So somebody knew, and somebody saw

And somebody heard your cries

Which you screamed out, but kept secret

And as I get out now, and walk forward

The chasm ahead is dark

The mist blows away in the wind from the north country

Yet still clings to my heart as the hollow sounds echo across the desolate rocks

And I will remember how I reached out across so many years

And touched your heart

And told you to live when you thought you couldn't

And you will remember my touch in its tenderness

And my hurt in its pain

And the cold wind which I sent in your heart

And I will remember your loveliness and your loneliness

As I lie in my darkness

And I will remember you and our love for always

www.ingramcontent.com/pod-product-compliance
Lightning Source LLC
Chambersburg PA
CBHW020014050426
42450CB00005B/463